W9-BHL-625

Pebble® Plus

How to Build a Tornado in a Bottle

Hands-On SCIENCE FUN

by Lori Shores

Consulting Editor: Gail Saunders-Smith, PhD

Consultant: Ronald Browne, PhD
Department of Elementary & Early Childhood Education
Minnesota State University, Mankato

CAPSTONE PRESS
a capstone imprint

Pebble Plus is published by Capstone Press,
151 Good Counsel Drive, P.O. Box 669, Mankato, Minnesota 56002.
www.capstonepub.com

Copyright © 2011 by Capstone Press, a Capstone imprint. All rights reserved.
No part of this publication may be reproduced in whole or in part, or stored in a retrieval system, or transmitted in any
form or by any means, electronic, mechanical, photocopying, recording, or otherwise, without written permission of the
publisher. For information regarding permission, write to Capstone Press,
151 Good Counsel Drive, P.O. Box 669, Dept. R, Mankato, Minnesota 56002

Books published by Capstone Press are manufactured with paper
containing at least 10 percent post-consumer waste.

Library of Congress Cataloging-in-Publication Data
Shores, Lori.
  How to build a tornado in a bottle / by Lori Shores.
    p. cm.—(Pebble Plus. Hands-on science fun)
  Summary: "Simple text and full-color photos instruct readers how to build a tornado in a bottle and explain the science
behind the activity"—Provided by publisher.
  Includes bibliographical references and index.
  978-1-4296-4493-8 (library binding)
  978-1-4296-5577-4 (paperback)
  1. Tornadoes—Experiments—Juvenile literature. I. Title. II. Series.
  QC955.2.S54 2011
  551.55'3078—dc22   2010013585

Editorial Credits
Jenny Marks, editor; Juliette Peters, designer; Laura Manthe, production specialist; Sarah Schuette;
    photo shoot direction; Marcy Morin, scheduler

Photo Credits
All photos by Capstone Studio: Karon Dubke except: Dreamstime: Chris White, 17; Shutterstock: Jhaz Photography,
    cover, back cover (background), 1, 2–3, 22, 23, 24, Rafai Fabrykiewicz, 4–5

Note to Parents and Teachers

The Hands-On Science Fun set supports national science standards related to physical science.
This book describes and illustrates building a tornado in a bottle. The images support early
readers in understanding the text. The repetition of words and phrases helps early readers learn
new words. This book also introduces early readers to subject-specific vocabulary words, which
are defined in the Glossary section. Early readers may need assistance to read some words and to
use the Table of Contents, Glossary, Read More, Internet Sites, and Index sections of the book.

Printed in the United States of America in North Mankato, Minnesota.
022011   006080R

CENTRAL ARKANSAS LIBRARY SYSTEM
SIDNEY S. McMATH BRANCH LIBRARY
LITTLE ROCK, ARKANSAS

Table of Contents

Safety Note:
Please ask an adult for help in building your tornado in a bottle.

Getting Started

The rain pours

and the wind roars.

Tornadoes can be scary.

But there's nothing scary

about a tornado in a bottle.

Here's what you need:

2 clear 2-liter plastic
bottles, clean

duct tape

3 cups (¾ liter) of water

blue food coloring

5

Making a Tornado in a Bottle

First, remove the labels from two 2-liter bottles. Then mix a few drops of food coloring into 3 cups (¾ liter) of water. Pour the colored water into one of the bottles.

Place the empty bottle
upside-down on top
of the first bottle.
Line up the openings.

Use duct tape to cover
the necks of the bottles.
Wrap the tape tightly
so the bottles
won't come apart.

Turn the bottles over
so the water is on top.
Watch as the water moves
slowly to the bottom.

Turn the bottles over again.

Quickly swirl the bottles
in a circle a few times.
Watch as a tornado appears!

How Does It Work?

Real tornadoes happen

when hot air pushes up.

Wind whips around

a center point,

pulling cold air down.

The tornado in the bottle works
in a similar way. When the
bottles are turned over,
the air pushs up.

air

Swirling the bottles around

makes the water spin

around the center hole.

Like wind, the movement pulls

the water down.

Glossary

roar—to make a loud, deep noise

similar—alike

swirl—to quickly move around in circles

whip—to quickly move with great force

Read More

Gibbons, Gail. *Tornadoes!* New York: Holiday House, 2009.

VanCleave, Janice. *Janice VanCleave's Big Book of Play and Find Out Science Projects.* New York: Jossey-Bass, 2007.

Internet Sites

FactHound offers a safe, fun way to find Internet sites related to this book. All of the sites on FactHound have been researched by our staff.

Here's all you do:

Visit *www.facthound.com*

Type in this code: 9781429644938

Index

Word Count: 185
Grade: 1
Early-Intervention Level: 20